Macey's store.
Mexican chili chipotle
- Annalo seed (Anias 7800So)
-spanish Rice.

Pantry-Friendly
Mexican Cooking

Debbie,
May this cookbook inspire you
to cook from your pantry.
LeAnn

Pantry-Friendly
Mexican Cooking

Economical Ways to Stretch Your Budget Without Cutting Back On Flavor

LeAnn Bird

Outskirts Press, Inc.
Denver, Colorado

Outskirts Press, Inc.
http://www.outskirtspress.com

ISBN: 978-1-4327-4016-0

Library of Congress Control Number: 2009938907

Outskirts Press and the "OP" logo are trademarks belonging to Outskirts Press, Inc.

PRINTED IN THE UNITED STATES OF AMERICA

Table of Contents

Mexican Cooking

It is strange to me that I have a passion for Mexican cooking, let alone being able to cook at all. Years ago, I could barely boil water and keep it from burning the pan. My mom was an excellent candy maker. She could whip up a batch of blue ribbon divinity or peanut brittle that was pleasing to the eye and tasted divine. She always made it look so easy. I thought if she could do it, so could I. I remember the first time l tried to make peanut brittle. It was a huge disaster! My pan permanently ruined with this black sugar substance that in no way resembled the peanut brittle my mother ever made. Finally, after several attempts to clean the pan, I threw it away and never mentioned my failure to anyone.

My next cooking attempt was to make Rice Krispies treats. Everyone said it was so easy. I followed the recipe and directions on the back of the cereal box perfectly. When the time came to cut the treats, I had a big surprise. I had created a new recipe: Rice Krispies rocks!

I was humiliated and ready to give up. Nevertheless, being stubborn and determined, knowing I could do it, I kept trying. I started slowly by trying basic recipes, attending cooking classes, reading cookbooks, asking questions of people who I thought were good cooks, watched cooking shows on TV, and finally after many years of trial and error, it happened. I could cook. It has become fun and very relaxing and has given me a wonderful sense of immediate accomplishment. The passion for cooking has inspired me to pursue my dream of sharing my favorite recipes.

As I was contemplating some of my favorite recipes, I realized they had everything to do with memories from my childhood, of growing up in Arizona, and spending time in the desert. I love the desert—it's beautiful, wild, arid, and yet so full of life. We were so close to Mexico that Mexican food became part of our lives. The tastes and flavors were new and fresh to me as a child and years later became my favorite.

My neighbors in Arizona introduced me to great Mexican cooking. They would spend days cooking in preparation for a fabulous dinner that was served following Christmas Mass. Intrigued by their custom to gather as family and friends and celebrate through the night, I thought what a great tradition; so I adapted their tradition and made it my own. Each Christmas season I invite my neighbors to a feast of my favorite Mexican recipes. I share new and favorites recipes that I have included in this cookbook. Every year I add a new twist or a new recipe. I appreciate my neighbors and friends for being great taste testers. Most recipes in this book have a little story of its origination. I hope my learning and love for cooking inspire you to try new recipes, cook more, and create your own traditions.

My cooking philosophy is:

By keeping a well-stocked pantry, you will save time and money. Every kitchen can prepare Mexican recipes with these basic ingredients. I like to keep these on hand for economical cooking in a rush. Using what I have stored I can prepare an intimate dinner for two or an elegant banquet for 20 without having to go to the store, make meals with ingredients from scratch, and save money by buying what is on sale.

Basic Ingredients
Tortillas - Corn & Flour
Canned or Dehydrated Refried Beans
Salsa
Cheese
Canned Green Chiles
Dried Chile Pods
Flour
Corn Masa
Rice
Canned Mexican Style Tomatoes
Vegetable Oil
Shortening or Lard
Canned Chipotles in Adobo Sauce

Basic Spices
Dried Cilantro
Cumin Powder
Garlic Powder
Oregano
Cayenne Pepper
Black Pepper
Peppercorns
Chipotle Seasoning
Annatto Seed
Paprika
Jalapeño Juice

If you have these basic ingredients, you can make a fabulous dish in minutes. Just add meat and you are ready for a quick and easy meal.

This great and easy recipe takes only minutes to prepare. I have made chimichangas and burritos for years and have had huge issues with the tortillas I bought at the store. When I folded the store-bought tortillas, it was hard to keep them from breaking. I had mentioned my dilemma to a coworker. She told me her husband worked as a chef at a Mexican restaurant, and that she would call him and ask him for advice. He produced this amazing and quick tortilla recipe. She translated the recipe and I wrote it all down onto a Post-it note.

Easy Homemade Flour Tortillas

- 1 cup flour
- 1 cup baking mix
- warm water (add a little at a time)

Mix all ingredients to form a play dough consistency and roll into small balls. Take the balls and roll out onto a floured board. Use a heavy rolling pin to roll dough into flat circles. Cook on a griddle until lightly browned; turn over and cook the other side. Use immediately for best results. Makes 8 8-inch tortillas.

Making tortillas by hand is an art and takes years of practice. I am all about shortcuts, so go out and get a good tortilla press. It makes good tortillas in an instant.

Corn Tortillas

- 1 cup corn flour masa
- ½ teaspoon salt
- warm water (add a little at a time)

Mix the ingredients until they are the consistency of soft play dough. Form into small balls. Press on tortilla press. Fry lightly on griddle. Makes 8 8-inch tortillas.

I have included instructions for two methods.

Roasting Green Chiles

Oven Method

Heat oven to 500 degrees. Spray cooking oil on a baking sheet. Place chiles on baking sheet and bake until the skin bubbles and turns black. Remove from baking sheet and place in a bowl with a moist towel over it. The steam will help the skins to slip off, and once you can handle them, gently peel off the skins.

BBQ Grill

Heat grill to 500 degrees. Place chiles directly onto the grill and roast until the skin bubbles and turns black. Remove from grill and place in a bowl with a moist towel over it. The steam will help the skins to slip off, and once you can handle them, gently peel off the skins.

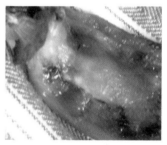

Roux is like a white sauce and can be used as a simple filling for enchiladas, burritos, and tacos when combined with meat.

Roux

- One large tablespoon of lard, shortening, or vegetable oil (I recommend using lard because it creates an authentic flavor.)
- ½ cup flour
- pinch red chili powder
- ¾ can meat stock
- ¾ cup shredded chicken, beef, or pork

Put oil into a medium saucepan and get it really hot; if it is near smoking it is just right. Add flour and remove from heat to blend. Add a pinch of red chili powder and cook until thick. Add stock. Blend into a smooth sauce and add shredded meat to the sauce. Add spices to season. Makes 1½ cups.

I love Chili Verde Sauce. It is great to pour over burritos, tamales, and tacos. It is a crowd pleaser when I serve it.

Chile Verde Sauce

- 1 large tablespoon shortening, lard, or vegetable oil
- 3-4 pork chops boned and cubed
- 1 large tablespoon flour
- 2 small cans green chiles (I like to use whole canned chiles so I can make the chunks larger or use fresh roasted chiles)
- 1 teaspoon cumin
- 4-5 cups chicken stock
- 2 tablespoons chopped cilantro

Drizzle oil in bottom of medium saucepan. Sprinkle pork cubes with flour and brown in the oil. Add the chiles, cumin, and chicken stock. Simmer mixture over medium heat for 1 -2 hours until it thickens. Add the cilantro just before serving. This sauce freezes well, if you by chance make enough to have leftovers. Makes 2 quarts.

This sauce is rich and smoky and a perfect accompaniment for meat dishes. It is great with Carne Asada and other grilled meats.

Adobe Sauce

- ¼ cup chopped dates or raisins
- 2 whole tomatoes, peeled and diced
- I chipotle pepper in adobe sauce
- I teaspoon cumin
- I teaspoon black pepper
- I tablespoon red cider vinegar
- ½ small onion, chopped
- ¼ cup olive oil
- juice of one lime
- I tablespoon honey or orange marmalade

In a food processor, pulse the ingredients. Cook in a small saucepan over medium heat until thick for a wonderful sauce accompaniment. Makes 1 cup.

I was making hotel reservations for a family trip, and struck up a conversation with the reservation agent about Mexican food. She shared with me one of her family's favorite recipes.

Chili de Aguila

- 1 15-oz. can of whole peeled tomatoes
- 2 garlic cloves, pressed
- 1 teaspoon oregano
- 1 teaspoon salt
- 1 teaspoon black pepper

Boil tomatoes with garlic and blend in a blender or food processor until it is a thin sauce. Add oregano, salt, and pepper just before grilling or baking. Makes 2 cups.

I prefer homemade to store-bought enchilada sauce, so I created my own recipe out of ingredients that I stock in my pantry. It comes in handy when you need to make a fabulous quick meal.

Enchilada Sauce

- 5-6 dried chile pods
- 2-3 cloves garlic, chopped
- 1 teaspoon cumin
- 1 teaspoon oregano
- 2 teaspoons salt
- 1 tablespoon sugar or honey
- ¾ teaspoon cinnamon
- 2 large cans tomato sauce
- 1 cup water (reserved from the chiles)

In a saucepan cover the chile pods with water and boil until soft. Save the water. Seed and stem the chiles. Add all ingredients in a food processor and blend. Transfer the mixture to a large pan with the tomato sauce and water and cook until the mixture thickens. The sauce will be thin. Makes 1 quart.

This is a great red sauce to use over meat dishes. I adapted the recipe of a good friend who owned a catering company. It is very simple and can be made in bulk and home canned for later use.

Chile Colorado Sauce

- 5 pods of dried New Mexico chiles (you can use what you have, but I love the red color of the New Mexico chiles). Boil the pods in water until they are soft. Cool slightly. Cut off the stems and seed the chiles.
- 1 teaspoon garlic powder
- 1 teaspoon cumin
- 1 teaspoon dried cilantro
- 1 stemmed and seeded Anaheim chile
- 1 small onion
- 1 bell pepper (I prefer the red or orange)
- 1 large can diced tomatoes
- 1 small can tomato paste
- 1 tablespoon cilantro
- salt and pepper (season to taste)

In a food processor puree the chile pods, garlic, cumin, cilantro, and Anaheim chile to form a smooth paste. Add and pulse to a chunky salsa texture. Add onion and bell pepper. Pulse again. Pour from food processor into a saucepan and add diced tomatoes, tomato paste. Heat the sauce through and season with salt and pepper. Add cilantro. Makes 1 quart.

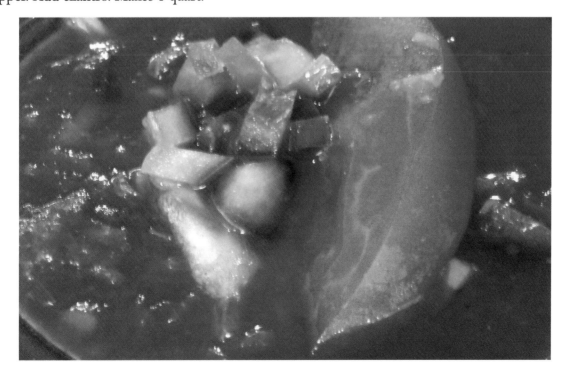

You can mix and store the spices for a quick seasoning right out of the cupboard. I like to use this rub when I am grilling for a special occasion.

Cumin Rub for Chicken or Fish

- 2 tablespoons olive oil
- 4 chicken breasts or fish fillets
- 1 teaspoon dried cilantro
- 2 teaspoons chili powder
- 2 teaspoons cumin
- 2 tablespoons garlic powder
- 1 tablespoon ground annatto seed
- 2 tablespoons fresh ground black pepper
- 1 teaspoon salt
- juice of 1 lime
- 1 lime cut into small pieces

Mix all dry ingredients. Set aside. Gently massage olive oil into meat. This will provide a base for the dry ingredients to stick to the meat. Spread the seasoning rub over the meat, coating all sides. Squeeze juice of the lime over meat just before serving. Garnish with lime segments.

In an effort to appeal to a wider range of taste preferences, I experimented with other options to create an onion-free salsa. In this version, I use peeled zucchini squash as the onion substitute.

Table Salsa

- I canned chipotle pepper in adobo sauce
- I jalapeño pepper (seeded and cut into ¼)
- I Anaheim chile (seeded and cut into ¼)
- I green bell pepper (seeded and cut into ¼)
- I Serrano pepper (seeded and cut into ¼)
- I peeled and cubed zucchini squash or I small onion
- 4 peeled tomatoes
- I tablespoon cumin
- I teaspoon salt
- 2 teaspoons of fresh cilantro
- I clove of garlic
- I tablespoon ground black pepper
- ¼ cup lime juice (fresh or bottled)

Put in food processor and blend until it is mixed. Not too much or you will get juice. If you want to have some on hand for later, follow the directions in a home canning guidebook for detailed instructions. Makes 1 quart.

I like to make this salsa fresh and chunkier than a regular table salsa.

Fresh Peach Salsa

- 1 jalapeño pepper (seeded and cut into ¼)
- 1 Anaheim chile (seeded and cut into ¼)
- 1 Serrano pepper (seeded and cut into ¼)
- ½ red or green sweet pepper (seeded and cut in ½)
- 4-5 canned peach halves
- 1 small onion
- 4 peeled tomatoes
- 1 tablespoon cumin
- 1 tablespoon kosher salt
- 2 tablespoons fresh cilantro
- 1 clove of garlic
- 1 tablespoon ground black pepper

Put all ingredients in a food processor and pulse until desired texture. Makes 1 quart.

My sweet version of Mango Salsa is so easy to make. You will be amazed at how well it enhances chicken or fish.

Mango Salsa

- ▪ I whole mango cut into chunks
- ▪ ¼ bunch fresh cilantro
- ▪ 2 jalapeño peppers, stemmed, seeded, and cut in half
- ▪ 4 Roma tomatoes, cut into ¼ pieces
- ▪ juice of 2 limes
- ▪ I teaspoon salt
- ▪ I yellow or red bell pepper, cut into ¼ pieces
- ▪ ½ small onion, cut into chunks

Put all ingredients into a food processor and pulse to the desired texture. I like to keep it a little chunky. Be careful not to over process. Store the salsa in the refrigerator. Makes 1 quart.

Fresh salsa is always a preferred choice of everyone. This recipe is so easy and a great addition to any Mexican dish.

Pico de Gallo

- ½ onion
- 1 jalapeño, seeded
- 1 Anaheim pepper, seeded
- 2 medium-sized tomatoes
- juice of 1 lime
- 1 teaspoon salt
- ½ teaspoon black pepper
- ½ teaspoon cumin
- 1 tablespoon cilantro, roughly chopped

Chop onion, jalapeño, pepper, and tomatoes into small pieces and place in small bowl. Add lime juice, seasonings, and cilantro. Toss together and serve. Makes 1 cup.

Quick and Easy Guacamole

- 2 ripe avocados mashed
- I cup sour cream
- 2 tablespoons salsa (anything that you have will work)

Mix together with a fork or food processor until creamy smooth. If it is going to sit awhile before serving, and to keep the guacamole from going brown, smooth a thin layer of mayonnaise over the top of the bowl. When you are ready to serve it, just mix in the mayonnaise. Makes 2 cups.

AVOCADO PREPARATION

The easiest way to peel and mash an avocado is to cut it in half and open the fruit. Pull out the seed. Leave meat in the skin. Using a knife, make cube-like cuts and then use a spoon to scoop out. Smash the pieces with a fork.

 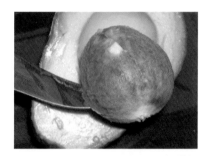 

Traditional Guacamole

- 2 ripe avocados mashed
- 1 teaspoon minced onion
- 1 teaspoon garlic powder
- ½ teaspoon chili powder
- ¼ teaspoon salt
- 1/3 cup of mayonnaise

Blend really well and just before serving add mayonnaise. Makes 1 cup.

During lunch the executive chef of a prestigious hotel and I discussed basic sauce recipes. Later I tested them, and then added my own twist. The tangy and rich flavors will add intensity to any meat dish.

Balsamic Glaze

- 2 cups sugar
- ½ cup balsamic vinegar
- ½ cup lime juice

Cook until sugar dissolves and mixture slightly thickens. Makes 1 cup.

This glaze is fantastic on pork or chicken.

Hot and Spicy Glaze

- I cup apricot jam
- I cup mayonnaise
- I tablespoon jalapeño juice

Cook until thickens. Makes 1 cup.

Sprinkle dressing on salad greens or use as a marinade for chicken recipes.

Cilantro Lime Vinaigrette

- ½ cup olive oil
- ¼ cup lime juice
- 2 tablespoons honey
- 4 tablespoons fresh rough chopped cilantro
- 1 teaspoon salt

Using a food processor, mix all ingredients. Makes 1 cup.

My good friend, business associate, and I have been sharing recipes and business ideas for many years. She makes fabulous pies, marinades, and salads. This recipe is no exception. She gets rave reviews every time she serves it. I think it is a great alternative to a traditional Avocado Dressing for chicken or pork.

Tomatillo Ranch Dressing

- 1 buttermilk ranch dressing packet (make dressing according to directions on the packet)
- 2 tomatillos, peeled
- ½ bunch cilantro
- 1 garlic clove
- juice of 1 lime
- 1 jalapeño, seeded and stem removed
- 1 teaspoon vinegar

Blend in a food processor until creamy and smooth. Makes 1 quart.

This is a great sauce to use layered on a bed of salad greens, or over rice. I adapted a basic fruit sauce by adding green chiles. I am sure you will love the taste too. My family likes to layer it with cheese, rice, ranch beans, and tomatoes.

Sweet Fruit Sauce for Chicken or Pork

- 1 cup sugar
- 1 cup red cider vinegar
- ½ cup Worcestershire sauce
- 4 cups chopped fruit (apricots, pineapple, peaches, mangos, etc.)
- 1 small can green chiles, diced
- 2 cups shredded chicken or pork

Cook sugar, vinegar, and Worcestershire sauce until sugar dissolves in a medium saucepan. Add fruit and simmer until thickens. Add green chiles. Stir in meat to create fantastic burritos or salads. Makes 2 cups.

I like Gazpacho Soup as a sauce for Shrimp Shooters. It is a fun base for a fabulous appetizer.

Shrimp Shooters with Gazpacho

- 12 large shrimp, cooked and peeled
- 12 celery stalks, cut to about 4 inches
- 12 lemon slices
- 4 cups gazpacho soup, divided

Add ¼ cup of gazpacho to the bottom of a tumbler glass. Stand a stalk of celery upright in the glass. Hang a large cooked shrimp on the rim of each glass. Garnish with lemon slice. Serves 12.

My family and I love to have breakfast burritos when we are camping or boating at the lake. It is easy to heat through on a camp stove or in a microwave oven.

Breakfast Burritos

- 1 pound of ground sausage
- 1 bag of shredded hash browns
- 6 eggs
- 1 cup cubed cheese
- 1 dozen large flour tortillas (heat part of the stack at a time in the microwave to soften for about 40 seconds)

Cook the sausage in little chunks until done in a fry pan. Drain grease and set aside in a large bowl. Using the same fry pan, add potatoes and cook until heated through. Once the potatoes are cooked, remove from pan and mix together with the sausage, previously set aside. Scramble the eggs and add to the sausage and potato mixture. Add the cheese and gently mix ingredients together. Take a large softened flour tortilla and add enough filling to cover the tortilla like a pizza pie. Roll up each end and then the center like a burrito. These are great to freeze and use later. Serves 12.

I was at the nearby convenience store getting a soft drink, and while waiting in line to pay for my drink this woman started complaining about her job to the manager behind the counter. She abruptly turned around to me and asked what I did for a living; apparently, I looked like I had a good job. I told her that I was a freelance meeting planner and was writing a Mexican cookbook. Fascinated by this she got excited. She then asked me if I had Birria in my cookbook. I said, "No," and asked her, "What is Birria?" She then explained that her ex-husband was from Mexico and this recipe came from his aunt. She did not know what part of Mexico it originated from, but she thought his family was from somewhere in central Mexico. I thought the recipe sounded interesting and asked if she would leave a copy with the store manager so I could try it. I left the store thinking that was an interesting encounter. A few days later, I went back to the same store. To my surprise, the manager came running out of her office to deliver me a copy of the handwritten recipe. I reviewed the recipe and realized I had all the ingredients right in my pantry. I immediately went to my kitchen and tested it out. What a pleasant surprise! You never can tell where and when you will discover a great recipe.

Birria Chicken

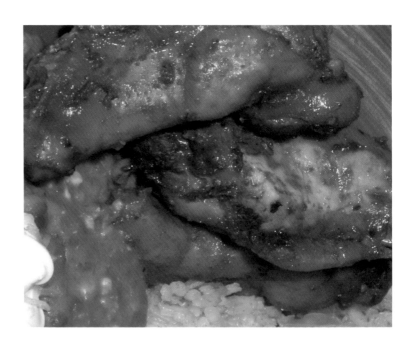

- 5 dried chile pods
- ¼ teaspoon garlic
- 1 teaspoon cumin
- 2 whole cloves
- 31 peppercorns balls
- 2 teaspoons oregano
- 1 teaspoon salt
- 2-3 pounds thawed chicken
- 5 dried bay leaves

Boil the dried chile pods until the pods are soft. Reserve the water. Cool the pods slightly. Remove the stem and seed the chiles. Put all ingredients into a food processor and grind into a paste. Add the chile water and blend in the food processor until it resembles a thin sauce. Pour over chicken and marinate in the refrigerator for at least 2 hours. Place in a baking dish and top with 5 bay leaves prior to baking. Bake chicken in sauce at 375 degrees for approximately 35 minutes, or until the chicken is cooked. Serves 8.

On vacation in Bahia Kino, Mexico, my husband and I had a great experience of sampling the fresh crab caught from the Sea of Cortez. I created a quick and easy recipe to enjoy anytime.

Crabmeat Tostadas

- 12 crispy tostada shells
- 3 cups cooked crabmeat, divided
- juice of 4 limes
- 1 teaspoon salt
- 1 teaspoon black pepper

Combine crabmeat with lime, salt, and pepper. Place on tortilla and garnish with thinly sliced cabbage, tomato, and lime juice. Serves 6

You can always make dinner spectacular with this quick and easy recipe made with ingredients right out of the pantry.

Refried Bean Tostada

- 1 dozen fresh corn tortillas
- 1 tablespoon of lard, shortening, or vegetable oil
- 1 15-oz. can of refried beans (vegetarian style is best)
- ½ cup shredded cheese
- 2 teaspoons garlic powder
- 1 15-oz. can pinto beans drained

In a shallow pan, fry corn tortillas until crispy and slightly browned. In a saucepan, heat oil until very hot and add beans. Stir until smooth. Add cheese and pinto beans. Carefully heat to simmer and let it simmer until warmed through. Top the tortilla with refried beans mixture. Garnish with sliced cabbage or lettuce, tomato, and salsa. Serves 6.

While working in Tucson, during corn harvest season I would join the throngs of people lined up at a local restaurant to partake of the green corn tamales. They were the tastiest tamale I had ever eaten. I searched everywhere for a recipe. I bought a cookbook because a Green Corn Tamale recipe was in the book. I tried the recipe but something was missing. It was not the same flavor, I remember. Over the years, I have experimented with different ingredients and cooking methods, and I think I have figured it out, finally. I buy frozen new white corn in a bag and it is a great substitute for the corn on the cob. It actually is easier to work with and I think it tastes the same.

Green Corn Tamales

- 1 16-oz. bag of frozen white sweet corn (thawed and drained)
- 2 cups corn flour masa
- 2 cups lard or shortening
- 2 cups longhorn cheese, shredded
- 2 tablespoons sugar
- 12 Anaheim chiles (can be whole canned)
- 2 dozen corn husks

In food processor, grind the corn. Add the masa and shortening, and blend to form a thick, creamy paste. If the mixture gets too thick, thin it out with a little milk. Add sugar and cheese and blend. Then you are ready for the assembly. Soak the corn husks in warm water and pat them dry with a paper towel. This makes them more pliable to work with. Take a large spoon or rubber spatula and spread the masa on the husk until it is evenly covered. Leave the ends free of masa. Add 2 small strips of green chile and fold up like a burrito, folding the ends into the sides. I like to make my green corn tamales in little pouches so as not to confuse them with the meat tamales. If you are having trouble making it stay together, you can use some of the masa as glue to hold it together. Repeat until all masa is used. Makes 24 tamales.

To cook the tamales, steam them in a large steamer pot for about 30 minutes or until the masa has set up and the husks easily pull away.

While living in Arizona, the neighborhood ladies taught my mom and me how to make tamales after my mom taught our next-door neighbor how to make apricot jam. This recipe originated from the neighborhood.

Meat Tamales

CORN MIXTURE

- 6 cups corn flour masa
- 2 cups lard or shortening
- 2 teaspoons salt
- 3 ½ cups water

Add water to masa. Beat lard until creamy and add to masa. Beat with an electric mixer to consistency of cream. Cover and set aside.

FILLING

- 1 lb of beef and pork roast
- 5 dried red chiles
- 1 small can jalapeño tomato sauce
- 2 tablespoons oregano
- 2 tablespoons garlic powder
- 1 tablespoon cumin

Cook roast until tender in a Crock-Pot. Fork shred meat. Set aside. Boil dried chiles in medium saucepan until they plump up and are soft. Reserve the liquid and set aside. Cool chiles slightly to seed and take the stem off. Cut chiles in large chunks and chop in a food processor. In a bowl, mix together with tomato sauce, oregano, garlic powder, and cumin. Add chiles and tomato sauce to the meat mixture and stir until all the ingredients are incorporated.

CORN HUSK WRAPS

- 3 dozen corn husks

Soak corn husks in water until soft, and dry them off. Spread the corn mixture onto a husk by holding it in your hand and spreading the mixture like you are buttering a piece of bread. Place a spoonful of the meat mixture in the center and fold the husk together. Fold the ends over each other so it seals the mixture. You can also take pieces of husks torn into small ribbons and tie up each end of the tamale. Steam the tamales for about 30 minutes or until the masa mixture is set. Serve with Chile Colorado or Verde Sauce. I have a large steam pot that I use to keep the water off the tamales. Makes 3 dozen.

An abundant crop of apricots ignited a passion. This recipe honors this great exchange of service among neighbors and lifelong friends.

Apricot Pineapple Jam

- 5 cups fresh ripe apricots
- 1 20-oz. can pineapple chunks (drained)
- 8 cups sugar
- ¼ cup lemon juice
- 1 teaspoon kosher salt

In food processor mix pitted apricots and pineapple, and pulse to desired consistency. Jam is supposed to have pieces of fruit so do not over process. In a large pan, add the sugar, lemon juice, and the fruit mixture. Over medium heat dissolve the sugar and then bring to a boil. Cook at a full rolling boil for 5-7 minutes. Pour into jars and seal. Jam will keep in the refrigerator for a couple of weeks. It can be home preserved to enjoy longer. Follow directions in home canning books.

This is the first recipe I perfected. It resembles a Quiche.

Chile Relleno Casserole

- 1 lb. or 2 cups shredded chicken
- 1 large onion
- 1 lb. cheddar cheese (chopped into cubes) divided
- 3 small cans green chiles
- 4 eggs
- 1 ½ cups milk
- ¼ cup flour
- pinch of salt and pepper

Cook onion until it is tender. Mix onion with chicken. Place chiles, chicken, and cheese in the bottom of a 9 x 13 baking dish. Reserve some of cheese to spread on top. Mix together eggs, milk, flour, and seasonings and pour over the top of the chicken mixture. Top with the extra cheese. Bake in oven for 35-40 minutes at 350 degrees. Serves 8-10.

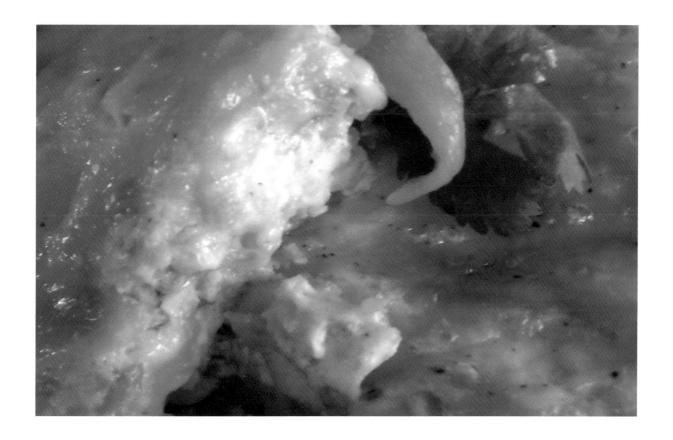

I love fajitas. They are easy to eat, made with healthy ingredients, and grilled to perfection. Add rice, guacamole, cheese, and salsa to a tortilla for a quick, healthy meal.

Chicken Fajitas

- 1 ½ lbs. chicken breast (skinless, boneless, and cut into strips)
- juice of 4 limes
- 2 tablespoons olive oil
- 2 tablespoons cumin
- 1 teaspoon dried oregano
- 1 teaspoon ground black pepper
- 1 teaspoon salt
- 2 large yellow onions (cut into strips)
- 1 each of yellow, red, green bell peppers cut into strips

Mix all ingredients and marinate overnight or for at least 2 hours. Drain, and grill until chicken is done and vegetables are tender. Place in warm flour tortilla and top with guacamole, cheese, Spanish rice, salsa, and sour cream. Serves 6-8.

Savory and full of healthy ingredients, this recipe will become one of your favorites.

Beef Fajitas

- 1 round steak cut into strips
- 2 tablespoons olive oil
- 3 tablespoons Worcestershire sauce
- 1 teaspoon coarse pepper
- 1 teaspoon salt
- 1 tablespoon oregano
- 1 clove of garlic (crushed)
- 2 large yellow onions (cut into strips)
- 1 each of yellow, red, green bell peppers cut into strips

Mix all ingredients and marinate overnight or for at least 2 hours. Drain, and grill until beef is done and vegetables are tender. Place in warm flour tortilla and top with guacamole, cheese, Spanish rice, salsa, and sour cream. Serves 6-8.

I had the privilege to attend a grand prix race weekend in Texas. In between the races, I struck up a conversation with a man from Mexico. We discussed the gastronomical delicacies from his hometown; many of the ingredients are too exotic or unavailable in my neighborhood grocery store. I prefer to make recipes with simple ingredients and instructions.

Easy Ground Beef Taco

- 1 lb. ground beef
- ½ cup salsa
- ¼ cup diced green peppers or onions
- 12 taco shells

Brown the ground beef into fine pieces. Cook the peppers and onions until tender. Add the salsa and heat through. Serve in taco shells with shredded lettuce, tomato, avocado slices, shredded cheese, and salsa. Serves 6.

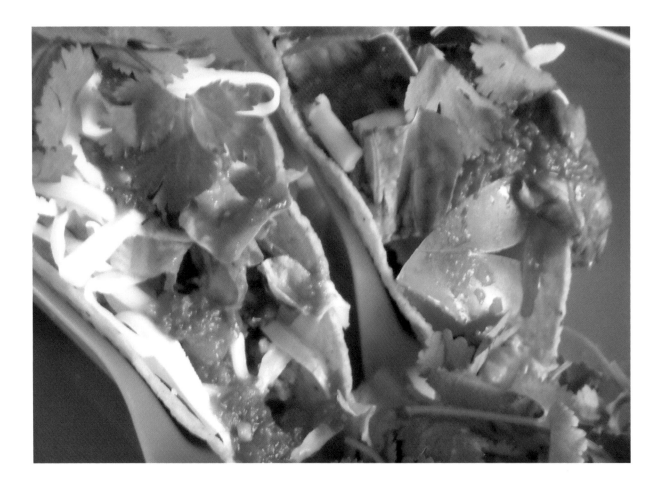

I was visiting with a friend before a concert and we started to discuss our favorite topic: food. He shared with me the most amazing miracle of how he bonded with his newly found aunt. An aunt married to an estranged uncle from Mexico showed up on his doorstep announcing that she wanted to meet her relatives and spend time with them before she was too old to travel. As they visited, they discovered that they both shared the love of cooking. He asked her to stay and teach him authentic recipes from her kitchen. She agreed to stay. He immediately took some time off work, spent about $200 a day in supplies and hours in the kitchen learning to cook her recipes, and getting to know this wonderful woman. They created many dishes together. He enjoyed her Carnitas the best. I took his basic recipe and created a Carnita that will melt in your mouth.

Carnitas

- 1 pound of pork roast
- 1 teaspoon cracked black pepper
- 2 teaspoons paprika
- 1 teaspoon chili powder
- 2 teaspoons garlic powder
- 1 cup chicken stock
- 1 cup orange juice
- 1 tablespoon of lard, shortening, or vegetable oil (I recommend using lard because it creates an authentic flavor)
- 1 dozen small flour tortillas

Mix all ingredients together and slow cook until the meat is tender enough to slice. Reserve the juices. Slice the meat into strips about 2 inches long and 1 inch wide. In a large fry pan heat the lard until it is hot. Add the meat and fry until slightly crispy. Remove meat from fry pan and drain on a paper towel lined plate. In a saucepan, place the reserved juices and the drained meat and boil until it is tender for about 1 hour. To serve place meat in a flour tortilla with sliced avocado, tomatoes, cheese, and sliced cabbage. Serves 4-6.

In a little village near Santo Tomas, while shopping for fresh produce, we met Anna, who was kind enough to interpret and introduce us to a few of the villagers. As we visited under the big shade tree outside the store, the conversation turned to Ceviche. Ceviche is the perfect meal on a hot summer day. It is cool and refreshing. She told me that she had the easiest recipe and was willing to share it with me. It was perfect timing since we had just bought fresh shrimp at the nearby fish market. I left with the rest of the ingredients to make my own Ceviche.

Shrimp Ceviche

- 1 cup raw shrimp peeled and deveined
- 2 cups water, reserve
- 1 whole cucumber, diced
- 1 whole tomato, diced
- 1 jalapeño pepper, seeded and diced
- 1 canned Anaheim chile, diced
- 1 avocado, peeled, seeded, and diced
- ½ red or yellow bell pepper, diced
- juice of 4 limes
- 1 teaspoon garlic powder
- ¼ bunch of fresh cilantro, chopped
- 1 teaspoon dried crushed chile peppers
- ½ cup of ketchup
- ½ teaspoon salt
- ½ teaspoon black pepper
- ¼ cup reserved shrimp water
- 1 dozen tostada shells

In a small saucepan, heat the water and boil the shrimp until it barely turns pink. Quickly remove from heat and drain. Reserve the water. While the shrimp cools, chop the vegetables and place in a medium-sized bowl. Chop the shrimp and add to the bowl. Add the ketchup, salt, and pepper. Pour the water over the mixture and stir together. Cover the mixture and chill in the refrigerator. To serve place a large spoonful on a tostada shell. Serves 4-6.

One of the stops on a Mexican Riviera Cruise is Mazatlan, Mexico. My husband and I had missed lunch on the boat so we opted to take a taxi to the downtown area and have lunch at a "locals only" place. We found this fabulous bakery & restaurant and quickly scoped it out. The clientele was tourist free, mostly families and business people, so in we went. The food looked amazing. As we looked around to see what we should select, we picked what they were eating, Fish Tacos. What a good choice. They were so good and the service was impeccable. I wish I knew the name of the place that inspired me to create my own Fish Taco recipe. It was a great dining experience.

Fish Tacos

- ½ lb. salmon, cod, flounder, trout, or halibut, cut into strips about 1 ½ inches wide
- 1 cup flour
- 1 egg, beaten
- ½ cup water
- 1 teaspoon salt
- 1 teaspoon black pepper
- ½ teaspoon baking soda

Mix all ingredients and dip fish pieces into batter. Deep fry fish until fish is done and slightly brown. Place in a crispy corn tortilla and top with yogurt crème sauce, shredded cabbage, sliced tomato, diced peppers, and a squeeze of lime. Serves 4.

Yogurt Crème Sauce

- ½ cup plain yogurt
- ½ cup sour cream
- 1 teaspoon lime juice
- 1 teaspoon dill pickle juice
- ½ teaspoon cumin
- ½ teaspoon horseradish
- 1 teaspoon garlic powder
- 1 teaspoon onion powder
- 1 teaspoon dill weed
- 1 teaspoon fresh chopped cilantro
- 1 teaspoon cayenne pepper

Mix and chill. Serve with Fish Tacos. Makes 1 cup.

During a cooking class, I was taught how to make chimichangas. I appreciate the patience the instructor showed me. I struggled to get it just right. Everything about it seemed so hard, but years later, I have perfected and simplified it. Typically, I will make my own flour tortillas for this recipe because it is very hard to find a soft tortilla at the grocery store that will not break apart.

Shredded Beef Chimichangas

- 1 lb. round or flank steak
- 3 teaspoons garlic powder

Cook steak smothered with garlic powder in a Crock-Pot or pressure cooker. Cook until tender and meat shreds easily. Set aside.

ROUX
- 1 large tablespoon of lard, shortening, or vegetable oil (I recommend using lard because it creates an authentic flavor)
- ½ cup flour
- pinch red chili powder
- ¾ can meat stock
- 2 teaspoons oregano
- 1 teaspoon salt
- 1 teaspoon black pepper

Put oil into a medium saucepan and get it really hot; if it is near smoking, it is just right. Add flour and take off heat to blend. Add pinch chili powder to roux, cook until thick. Add meat stock and blend into a smooth sauce. Add shredded meat mixture to the sauce. Add oregano, salt, pepper. Set aside.

BEANS
- 1 large spoonful of lard, shortening, or vegetable oil (get very hot)
- 1 large can of refried beans (vegetarian style is best)
- ½ cup milk
- 1 teaspoon garlic powder
- ½ cup shredded cheese

Carefully heat to simmer and let simmer until heated through. Add cheese.

TO ASSEMBLE CHIMICHANGAS

- 12 8-inch flour tortillas, fresh made or store bought
- refried beans
- meat mixture
- 2 cups vegetable oil

Warm the flour tortillas by heating on griddle. Spread beans like sauce to the edges of the tortilla. Add about a tablespoon of meat mixture and spread to the edges. Roll once and then fold over each end to form a package. Secure with a toothpick as needed. In a large fry pan heat oil and place burrito gently in the oil and fry until golden brown. Carefully turn burrito over to fry other side. Drain on a paper towel covered plate. Top with lettuce, sour cream, cheese, and guacamole. Serves 6.

Chicken Chimichangas

- 1 lb. boneless, skinless chicken breasts
- 3 teaspoons garlic powder

Cook chicken smothered with garlic powder in a Crock-Pot or pressure cooker. Cook until tender and meat shreds easily. Set aside.

ROUX

- 1 large tablespoon of lard, shortening, or vegetable oil (I recommend using lard because it creates an authentic flavor)
- ½ cup flour
- pinch red chili powder
- ¾ can chicken stock
- 2 teaspoons cumin
- 1 teaspoon salt
- 1 teaspoon black pepper

Put oil into a medium saucepan and get really hot; if it is near smoking, it is just right. Add flour and take off heat to blend. Add pinch chili powder to roux, cook until thick. Add chicken stock and blend into a smooth sauce. Add shredded meat mixture to the sauce. Add oregano, salt, pepper. Set aside.

BEANS

- 1 large spoonful of lard, shortening, or vegetable oil (get very hot)
- 1 large can of refried beans (vegetarian style is best)
- ½ cup milk
- 1 teaspoon garlic powder
- ½ cup shredded cheese
- Carefully heat to simmer and let simmer until heated through. Add cheese.

TO ASSEMBLE CHIMICHANGAS

- 12 8-inch flour tortillas, fresh made or store bought
- refried beans
- meat mixture
- 2 cups vegetable oil

Heat the tortillas on a griddle to make them pliable. Spread beans like sauce to the edges of the tortilla. Add about a tablespoon of meat mixture and spread to the edges. Roll once and then fold over each end to form a package. Secure with a toothpick as needed. In a large fry pan heat oil and place burrito gently in the oil and fry until golden brown. Carefully turn burrito over to fry other side. Drain on a paper towel covered plate. Top with lettuce, sour cream, cheese, and guacamole. Serves 6.

Shredded Pork Chimichanga

- 1 lb. pork roast
- 3 teaspoons garlic powder

Cook pork smothered with garlic powder in a Crock-Pot or pressure cooker. Cook until tender and meat shreds easily. Set aside.

ROUX

- 1 large tablespoon of lard, shortening, or vegetable oil (I recommend using lard because it creates an authentic flavor)
- ½ cup flour
- pinch red chili powder
- ¾ can meat stock
- 2 teaspoons oregano
- 1 teaspoon salt
- 1 teaspoon black pepper

Put oil into a medium saucepan and get really hot; if it is near smoking, it is just right. Add flour and take off heat to blend. Add pinch chili powder to roux, cook until thick. Add meat stock and blend into a smooth sauce. Add shredded meat mixture to the sauce. Add oregano, salt, pepper. Set aside.

BEANS

- 1 large spoonful of lard, shortening, or vegetable oil (get very hot)
- 1 large can of refried beans (vegetarian style is best)
- ½ cup milk
- 1 teaspoon garlic powder
- ½ cup shredded cheese

Carefully heat to simmer and let simmer until heated through. Add cheese.

TO ASSEMBLE CHIMICHANGAS

- 12 8-inch flour tortillas, fresh made or store bought
- refried beans
- meat mixture
- 2 cups vegetable oil

Warm the flour tortillas by heating on griddle. Spread beans like sauce to the edges of the tortilla. Add about a tablespoon of meat mixture and spread to the edges. Roll once and then fold over each end to form a package. Secure with a toothpick as needed. In a large fry pan heat oil and place burrito gently in the oil and fry until golden brown. Carefully turn burrito over to fry other side. Drain on a paper towel covered plate. Top with lettuce, sour cream, cheese, and guacamole. Serves 6.

Everyone asks me, "Do you have a good mole?" I really did not. After answering this question so many times that I lost track, I succumbed to the peer pressure and created a "mole" recipe that is easy and tastes great. I have used the ingredients that are grown in areas of Northern Mexico and Southern Arizona. It easily freezes for a quick out-of-the-freezer meal in minutes.

Sweet Mole

- 8-10 dried or fresh chiles (any variety will do, I use a combination and mostly the mild varieties)
- 6 tablespoons of vegetable oil
- ¾ cup water
- 2 teaspoons onion powder
- I diced garlic clove
- I medium Roma tomato, cut into sections
- 2 pieces toasted whole wheat bread, cut in cubes
- 2 tablespoons chopped dates
- 2 tablespoons shelled pecans
- ½ teaspoon ground cinnamon
- ¼ teaspoon cloves
- 2 oz. melted Xocai™ Nuggets (dark chocolate)
- ¼ cup honey
- salt to taste
- 3-4 cups chicken broth
- 3 lbs. chicken breasts

Remove stem and seeds from the chiles and fry in 3 tablespoons of the oil until tender. In a food processor, blend the chiles and water to form a paste. Add all ingredients except the broth and blend to a thick sauce. If it gets too thick, add some of the broth to make it thinner. Transfer the blended sauce into a heavy saucepan and add the rest of the broth. Simmer for 1 ½ hours until thick and all the flavors are incorporated. It will smell wonderful. Pour sauce over chicken and bake at 350 degrees for 30 minutes. Serves 6.

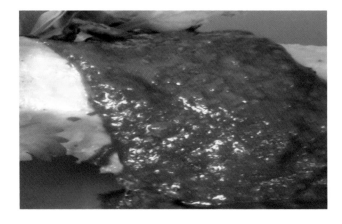

Carne Asada is grilled meat that simply melts in your mouth. While traveling in Mexico we followed a recommendation to try the Carne Asada at a restaurant in Caborca. What an Excellent recommendation! I love to serve the meat in small flour tortillas with grilled vegetables, Adobe Sauce or salsa.

Carne Asada

- 1 lb. skirt steak or flank steak

MARINADE

- 1 teaspoon cumin
- 1 teaspoon coarse pepper
- ¼ cup olive oil
- ¼ cup balsamic vinegar
- 2 tablespoons Worcestershire sauce
- 1 tablespoon garlic powder
- 3 tablespoons brown sugar or honey
- 1 teaspoon coarse salt
- juice of 2 limes
- 2 teaspoons chipotle seasoning

Pour marinade over the meat and let stand in the refrigerator for at least 2 hours. Grill steak over high heat. Turn once and let it sit for a few minutes before slicing. Cut diagonally across the grain for more tender meat. Serve with Adobe Sauce and grilled vegetables. Serves 6.

During a weekend retreat with my mom, we were exploring the Donner Reed Museum near Truckee, California and stopped in a little deli for lunch. It was intriguing to see the variety of specialty salsas they sold as gift items. One especially caught my eye as a great flavor combination. It was a two-olive salsa. I bought a jar and tested the flavors. I loved the tang of the green olives and the mellow of the black. These flavor combinations inspired me to create a black bean enchilada recipe. I blended the black beans with the two olive salsa flavors.

Black Bean Enchiladas

- I cup cooked black beans
- 3 tablespoons garlic powder
- I cup chopped black olives
- I cup chopped green olives (use the salad kind, they don't have anything stuffed in them)
- I dozen white corn tortillas
- ½ cup warm vegetable oil
- I small can of whole green chiles, cut into ½ strips
- 2 lb. Monterey Jack cheese cut 8 oz. into ½ inch thick x 2-3 inch strips, divided, reserve
- 2 cups Chile Verde Sauce, recipe below
- I cup Monterey Jack cheese, reserved, shredded

Mix beans, garlic, olives. Set aside. In a small saucepan over low heat, warm the oil. Dip tortilla into oil; quickly drain onto paper towel covered plate. Place tablespoon of the bean mixture in the center of the tortilla. Add strip of chile and cheese. Roll up and repeat the process. Assemble the enchiladas in a 9 x 13 baking pan and pour a little of the Verde Sauce to cover the bottom of the dish. Pour remaining Chile Verde Sauce over the enchiladas and top with cheese. Bake at 350 degrees for 30 minutes. Serves 6.

Chile Verde Sauce

- 3 tablespoons vegetable oil
- 3 tablespoons flour
- I small can diced green chiles
- I teaspoon cumin
- I teaspoon garlic powder
- ½ teaspoon salt
- I teaspoon fresh cilantro, chopped
- 2 cups vegetable or chicken stock

Mix the shortening and flour to make a thick roux. Add the vegetable or chicken stock to blend into a creamy sauce. Add the rest of the ingredients and bring to a simmer. Set aside. Makes 2 cups.

My husband loves this version of chicken enchiladas. I can make a giant pan and they can be gone within a couple of days. I use corn tortillas because they do not get soggy like flour tortillas. The white sauce is a perfect change to the traditional red sauce.

Chicken Enchiladas

- 1 large tablespoon shortening, lard, or vegetable oil
- 1 large tablespoon flour
- 2 cups chicken stock (you may not need all of the stock so use and stir as you go; some days it takes more, some less)
- 1 small onion, diced
- 1 small can diced green chiles
- 2 teaspoons cumin
- 1 teaspoon garlic powder
- 1 teaspoon oregano
- 1 tablespoon dried cilantro
- 1 dozen white corn tortillas
- 1 cup cheddar cheese, shredded
- 2 tablespoons fresh cilantro, chopped
- 1 cup cooked chicken, diced or shredded

In a medium saucepan heat the shortening until hot and add the flour, stirring until it forms a roux. Carefully add the chicken stock and stir until thick. Add onions, green chiles, spices, and chicken into the roux mixture and heat through. Set aside.

SAUCE

- 1 can cream of chicken soup
- 1 small can diced green chiles
- 1 teaspoon cumin
- 1 teaspoon salt
- 1 teaspoon black pepper
- 1 teaspoon garlic powder

To create the sauce, blend the cream of chicken soup, green chiles, and spices. Spread sauce over the bottom of a 9 x 13 baking dish. Heat the tortillas until soft in a microwave or by dipping them into hot oil. Spread mixture onto the tortilla and roll it up. Place in the pan seam side down. Repeat until the pan is full. Pour the remaining sauce over the enchiladas and top with grated cheese and cilantro. Bake in a 350-degree oven for 30 minutes. For quick results cook enchiladas in a microwave for 12-15 minutes, adding the cheese the last 2 minutes. Serves 6.

It is always nice to have two versions of enchiladas: this one uses a red sauce.

Chicken Enchiladas

SAUCE
- 2 cups enchilada sauce, divided
- 1 small can diced green chiles
- 1 cup diced tomatoes (they can be fresh or canned; if using canned make sure they are drained)
- 1 dozen corn tortillas

FILLING
- 1 cup cooked chicken, diced or shredded
- 1 small can whole green chiles, cut into strips
- 1 cup longhorn cheese, shredded, divided

Mix enchilada sauce, chiles, and tomatoes in a bowl. Set aside. In a 9 x 13 baking pan add a little of the sauce to cover the bottom. Soften the tortillas before rolling by microwaving or dipping in warm oil to make them pliable. Place the tortilla in the baking pan and add a spoonful of chicken, strip of green chile, and a teaspoon of cheese. Roll up and repeat until the tortillas are all used. Spread remaining sauce over the enchiladas until they are covered. Add remaining cheese. Bake in a 350-degree oven for 30 minutes. For quick results cook enchiladas in a microwave for 12-15 minutes, adding the cheese the last 2 minutes. Serves 6.

Struggling with the question of what to have for dinner? This basic enchilada recipe will get you to a fantastic dish in just minutes. This recipe is from a friend who was on the run, with many young children, a husband pursuing a new career, and limited funds in their bank account. She was able to stretch her food budget and get a great meal in return.

Ground Beef Enchiladas

- 1 lb. ground beef
- 1 onion, chopped
- 1 small can diced green chiles
- 1 small can olives, chopped
- 1 cup cheese, shredded, divided
- 1 can of enchilada sauce or 1 cup of homemade sauce, divided
- 1 dozen corn tortillas

Brown the hamburger with the onion. Drain any excess grease and liquids. In a medium bowl, combine meat mixture with the chiles, olives, and 1/2 of the cheese. Warm the sauce in a saucepan. Spread a small amount of the sauce in the bottom of a 9 x 13 baking pan. Dip a tortilla in sauce, add a large spoonful of filling, roll the tortilla up, and place in pan with seam side down. Repeat until all filling and tortillas are used. Pour any remaining sauce over the enchiladas and top with the rest of the grated cheese. Bake in a 350-degree oven for about 30 minutes or in a microwave oven for 10-12 minutes. Serves 6.

This is a pure and basic recipe. I have adapted it by using a variety of cheeses.

Cheese Enchiladas

- I can or I cup of enchilada sauce, divided
- I dozen white corn tortillas
- ½ lb. cheese (any combination of Monterey Jack, cheddar, cotija Mexican cheese). Cut into strips of ¼ inches wide by 3 inches
- I can whole green chiles (cut into strips about ¼ wide)
- I cup cheese, grated
- I tablespoon fresh cilantro, roughly chopped

Spread sauce in the bottom of a 9 x 13 baking dish. Heat the sauce in a small saucepan. Dip a tortilla in the sauce to soften and fill with cheese strip and a piece of green chile. Roll and place in the pan. Repeat until pan is full. Pour remaining sauce over the enchiladas and top with grated cheese and cilantro. Bake in a 350-degree oven for about 20 minutes. Serves 6.

Unexpected ingredients are a flavorful combination to tantalize your taste buds.

Chicken Quesadillas

- 2 large flour tortillas
- ½ cup cooked chicken, diced or shredded
- ¼ cup bacon bits
- 2 tablespoons cilantro, chopped
- 1/3 cup whole green chiles, cut into strips
- ½ cup white cheese, shredded

Place all ingredients on a large tortilla and top with cheese. Place the tortilla on hot griddle pan and top with additional tortilla. Grill until brown and cheese melts. Turn and brown on other side. Cool slightly and cut with a pizza cutter. Serve with guacamole and salsa. Serves 2.

My assistant was getting married and, in confidence, revealed to me that she needed help in the kitchen with some basic recipes. I thought it was a perfect office coworker's wedding gift. In secret, I requested easy favorite recipes from the staff. I got many great recipes for all kinds of foods. I compiled and bound a personalized newlywed cookbook for her. This was a favorite of mine and could be adapted to use as a quick filling for an enchilada, taco, or burrito.

Shrimp Quesadillas

- 2 tablespoons olive oil
- I small onion, thinly sliced
- I garlic clove, minced
- ½ cup frozen peas, thawed
- I small red bell pepper, cut in strips
- I Roma tomato, cut in rounds
- I teaspoon chipotle seasoning
- ½ cup water or stock
- 2 cups thawed or fresh shrimp, peeled and deveined
- I dozen flour tortillas
- I cup cheese, shredded

In a medium sauté pan, heat olive oil and then add onions and garlic. Sauté mixture for about 2 minutes. Add peas, bell peppers, and tomato and sauté for another 2-3 minutes. Add seasoning to taste and then add the water or stock. Bring sauce to a boil and add peeled shrimp. Cook no longer than 3 minutes; shrimp will turn pink when cooked. Do not overcook the shrimp; it will make it tough.

QUESADILLAS PREPARATION

Place tortillas on flat surface, sprinkle with cheese, and add some of the shrimp mixture. Then add more cheese to glue it together. Place another tortilla over the mixture. Cook it on a griddle or frying pan and toast the quesadillas until crispy and slightly brown. Serve warm with sour cream or guacamole. Serves 6.

My dad loves Chile Relleno and orders it everywhere. Many of the recipes turned out to be more like scrambled eggs with green chiles, which was not exactly what his taste buds were craving. I decided to create a recipe that my dad would love. Now he just asks, "When are you going to make me Chile Relleno?" At least he is not disappointed anymore. You can use any type of chile, but I like to use either an Anaheim or poblano pepper. You will want peppers that are long and have some space in the middle for the filling.

Meat Stuffed Chile Relleno

FILLING

- 6 poblano or Anaheim peppers, fire roasted
- 1 cup cooked beef, chicken, or pork
- ½ cup stock
- 1 teaspoon cumin
- 1 teaspoon garlic
- 1 teaspoon oregano
- ½ finely diced jalapeño
- 1 egg
- 1 piece of whole wheat toast

Heat an oven to 500 degrees. Spray cooking oil on a baking sheet. Place chiles on baking sheet and bake until the skin bubbles and turns black. Remove from baking sheet and place in a bowl with moist paper towels over it. The steam will help the skins to slip off, and once you can handle them, gently peel off the skins, being careful not to tear the sides. Cool slightly. Cut a single line up the side of the pepper and take out the seeds. Leave the stem on for easy handling. Set aside. In a food processor, grind all ingredients but peppers into a thick paste. Fill the peppers with the meat paste by carefully placing the filling through the slit side without tearing the pepper.

EGG WHITE BATTER

- 2 egg whites, beat until foamy
- 1 teaspoon cream of tartar
- 1 teaspoon salt
- 1 teaspoon black pepper

Place filled peppers carefully in the egg batter coating entirely. Deep fry the peppers in hot oil 375 degrees in a shallow pan until golden brown. Drain on paper towel lined plate. Serve with Chile Verde or Chile Colorado Sauce. Serves 6.

You can use any type of chile but I like to use either an Anaheim or poblano pepper. You will want peppers that are long and have some space in the middle for the filling.

Cheese Stuffed Chile Relleno

FILLING

- 6 poblano or Anaheim peppers, fire roasted
- 3 oz. cream cheese
- I cup shredded cheese
- I egg
- I piece of toast
- I teaspoon cumin
- I teaspoon dry mustard
- I teaspoon dried cilantro
- I teaspoon ground chili powder

Heat an oven to 500 degrees. Spray cooking oil on a baking sheet. Place chiles on baking sheet and bake until the skin bubbles and turns black. Remove from baking sheet and place in a bowl with moist paper towels over it. The steam will help the skins to slip off, and once you can handle them, gently peel off the skins, being careful not to tear the sides. Cool slightly. Cut a single line up the side of the pepper and take out the seeds. Leave the stem on for easy handling. Set aside. In a food processor, grind all ingredients but peppers into a thick paste. Fill the peppers with the cheese mixture by carefully placing the filling through the slit side without tearing the pepper.

EGG WHITE BATTER

- 2 egg whites, beat until foamy
- I teaspoon cream of tartar
- I teaspoon salt
- I teaspoon black pepper

Place filled peppers carefully in the egg batter coating entirely. Deep fry the peppers in hot oil 375 degrees in a shallow pan until golden brown. Drain on a paper towel covered plate. Serve with Chile Verde or Chile Colorado Sauce. Serves 6.

Every time my family would go out to dinner at a local Mexican restaurant, my mother would inevitably order deep fried green chile burritos. Years later, I found out that she is not a fan of refried beans but loves chimichangas. This was a safe, yummy alternative for her.

Deep Fried Green Chile Burrito

ROUX

- 1 large tablespoon of lard, shortening, or vegetable oil (I recommend using lard because it creates an authentic flavor)
- ½ cup flour
- pinch of red chili powder
- ¾ can chicken stock
- 1 small can diced green chiles
- 1 teaspoon oregano
- 1 teaspoon salt
- 1 teaspoon pepper
- 1 cup Monterey Jack cheese, coarsely grated
- 6 medium-size flour tortillas

Heat oil into a medium saucepan and get really hot; if it is near smoking, it is just right. Add flour and take off heat to blend. Add red chili and cook until thick. Add chicken stock. Blend into a smooth sauce. Add green chiles to the sauce. Add oregano, salt, pepper. Place a layer of filling over the entire tortilla. Sprinkle with cheese. Roll up, folding in the sides and then finishing with the ends. Deep fry the burritos in a shallow pan at 375 degrees. Drain on paper towel lined plate. Serve immediately and top with guacamole, sour cream, shredded cheese, and salsa. Serves 6.

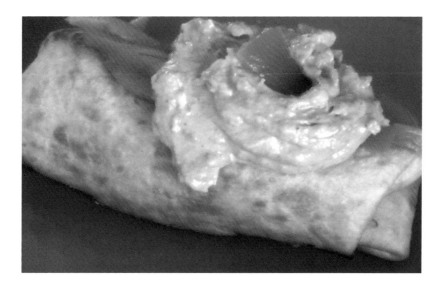

A neighbor gave this recipe to me; it is so quick and easy.

Arroz con Pollo (Rice & Chicken)

- 2 tablespoons olive oil
- ½ medium onion chopped
- ½ each of red and green peppers diced
- 1 garlic clove chopped
- 4 chicken breasts cut into small pieces
- 1 cup rice
- 2 cups chicken broth
- 2 cups water
- 1 cup frozen mixed vegetables
- 1 tomato diced
- ½ small can chopped olives (green or black)
- 2 tablespoons cilantro
- salt and pepper to taste

In olive oil sauté onions, peppers, and garlic until they are soft. Add chicken pieces and sauté the chicken until browned. Add the rice and cook the rice and chicken until the rice begins to brown. Add the chicken stock and 2 cups of water and cook covered until the rice is soft. Add frozen vegetables, olives, cilantro, and tomato just before serving. Add salt and pepper to taste. Serves 6.

Gazpacho is a traditional cold soup. I like to use mine as a base for Shrimp Shooters.

Gazpacho

- 4 large peeled and diced tomatoes — can use canned, drained, diced tomatoes
- 1 small cucumber
- 1 stalk of celery
- 1 small green pepper
- 1 Anaheim chile, stemmed and seeded
- 1 chipotle pepper in adobo sauce
- 1 small onion
- 1 minced garlic clove
- 1 tablespoon lemon juice
- 1 tablespoon vegetable oil
- 1 teaspoon salt
- 1 teaspoon pepper
- 2 cups of tomato or chicken stock

Combine all ingredients into a food processor and pulse into small pieces. Transfer to a medium pan, add the stock, and heat through. Chill before serving. Serves 4.

This is a twist on a classic taco soup recipe I got from a dear friend who made sure my kindergartner got to school every day. We were both building new homes in the same neighborhood and our boys were in the same class. We lived in apartments about 15 miles from the school, so we drove our children to school every day. For an unknown reason my son refused to go to school; he would cry, kick, scream, cling to the car door, and make both of our lives miserable. Well, my friend saved my son and me. She volunteered to take my boys to school and then I picked them up. It was a good carpool arrangement.

Pantry Taco Soup

- 1 ½ lb. ground beef
- 1 small can diced green chiles
- ½ cup chunky salsa
- 1 15-oz. can kidney beans, undrained
- 1 15-oz. can garbanzo beans, undrained
- 2 15-oz. cans stewed tomatoes, roughly chopped
- 2 cups beef broth
- ½ cup chopped olives

Brown meat and add chiles and salsa in large saucepan. Add the rest of the ingredients and heat through. Garnish with sour cream, shredded cheese, tortilla chips, and avocado pieces. Serves 6.

Have you ever had a really stressful day and somehow a nice bowl of soup calmed you down? I was out of town and had one of those days… On my way home, I had few minutes to get some food and found this fantastic soup at, of all places, the airport. This is how I remember it. I hope it brings you a calming feeling at the end of a stressful day like it did for me.

Chicken Green Chile Soup

- 3 tablespoons vegetable oil
- 3 tablespoons flour
- 3-4 cups chicken broth, divided
- 4 boneless chicken breasts, cut into small strips and sprinkled with garlic powder and cumin. Grill the chicken until cooked.
- 2 roasted Anaheim chiles, cut into medium pieces
- 1 small can diced green chiles
- 1 small onion diced
- 1 small can whole green chiles, cut into medium strips
- 1 teaspoon cumin
- 1 teaspoon black pepper
- ½ teaspoon adobe spice
- 1 teaspoon garlic powder
- 2 teaspoons fresh, roughly chopped cilantro
- juice of 2 limes

Mix vegetable oil and heat until hot; add flour and mix together until smooth. Remove from heat and add ½ of the broth to form a roux. Mix until smooth and then add the other ingredients. Soup will begin to thicken. Add the rest of the broth and the cilantro. Simmer for 30-45 minutes. Serves 8.

I was managing a meeting at a very prestigious resort in Arizona, and they served the best enchilada soup on the lunch buffet. I had been there for a few days and dared to ask the chef what his secret was to the great soup. He then gave me one of the best secrets I have never been able to keep. He reminded me about the enchiladas that were on the buffet menu yesterday and that his "secret" is to take the leftover enchiladas and blend in a food processor. Pulse to a desired consistency, add chicken stock, and heat through. I like to leave it a little chunky so you can tell what the various ingredients are. So now, the secret is out...

Enchilada Soup

- ½ pan leftover enchiladas
- 2 cups chicken broth

Pulse the enchiladas in a food processor until it is chunky smooth. Add stock to mixture. Heat through and serve. Garnish with sour cream, tortilla chips, and a sprinkle of cheese. Serves 6.

In our area, we had a tradition of playing Bunko once a month with the other women in the neighborhood. It started as a way to get to know your neighbors and turned into lasting friendships. We all took turns hosting a dinner and the game at our homes. This recipe is from one of my Bunko friends. I adapted her recipe to have a Mexican flavor.

White Chile Bean Soup

- 2 tablespoons olive oil
- I small onion, chopped
- I garlic clove, chopped
- 4 chicken breasts, boiled and shredded
- juice of I lime
- 3-4 cups chicken broth
- I cup water
- ½ cup frozen white corn
- 2 small cans chopped green chiles
- 2 15-oz. cans drained northern white beans
- I 15-oz. can drained garbanzo beans
- I small can white hominy
- I teaspoon cumin
- ½ teaspoon fresh ground pepper
- ½ teaspoon lemon pepper
- I teaspoon salt

In a large saucepan sauté the onion in olive oil until it is soft. Add garlic. Be careful not to burn the garlic. Add the rest of the ingredients and heat through. Serve with tortilla chips, shredded Monterey Jack cheese, or a dollop of sour cream. Serves 8.

During one of our trips to Mexico we had the privilege of spending time with this amazing man. Over dinner, he would share tidbits of Mexican culture, travel destinations, and food. One of his favorite recipes is Posole. I hope Chris likes my version of lean pork and chock-full-of-vegetables soup.

Posole

- 5 dried chile pods (I like the New Mexico chiles because they are a nice red color.) In small saucepan, boil chiles until tender. Reserve the water. Cool slightly then seed and stem pods.
- 3 garlic cloves
- 1 teaspoon sea salt
- 1 teaspoon pepper
- 1 teaspoon cumin
- 3 teaspoons fresh cilantro, rough chopped, divided
- juice of 3 limes
- 2 cups pork loin, cubed
- 3 tablespoons vegetable oil
- 1 29-oz. can white hominy
- 1 15-oz. can diced tomatoes
- 6 cups chicken or vegetable stock
- 3 cups potatoes, diced
- 1 cup carrot, diced
- 1 rib of celery, diced
- 2 cups green cabbage, loosely chopped

Pulse chiles, garlic, salt, pepper, cumin, 2 teaspoons cilantro, and lime juice in a food processor until it is smooth. Add reserved water if mixture becomes thick. In large pot, sear meat in vegetable oil on all sides. Add the processed ingredients, vegetables, and stock, and cook until vegetables are tender. Garnish with remaining chopped cilantro. Serves 8.

My family loves the creamy texture of this rice with everything.

Family Favorite Rice

- 1 cup rice
- 3 tablespoons olive oil
- 1 garlic clove, minced
- 1 small sweet pepper, diced (green, red, yellow, or chocolate)
- 4-5 cups chicken broth, fresh or canned
- ½ teaspoon salt
- 3-4 stewed tomatoes, chopped
- ½ cup frozen peas
- 1 teaspoon fresh cilantro, chopped
- 1 teaspoon cumin

Place rice in hot water and soak for 15 minutes. Drain and spread rice onto waxed paper to dry out evenly. Heat olive oil in a skillet and add garlic, pepper, and rice. Add chicken broth, salt, and tomatoes; cover and simmer for 30 minutes, stirring frequently to keep from sticking. Add peas, cilantro, and cumin, and continue to simmer for additional 10 minutes. If it starts to stick, stir in a little more chicken stock or water. Garnish with shredded cheese. Serves 6.

Mexican Vegetables

- 1 small- to medium-sized zucchini summer squash (cubed)
- 1 ear of fresh corn, cut off the cob
- 1 small red pepper, diced
- ¼ cup table salsa
- ½ teaspoon cumin
- 1 teaspoon fresh cilantro, roughly chopped
- ½ cup shredded cheese

Boil vegetables until tender. Add the salsa and cumin. Before serving, add cilantro and cheese. Serves 4.

My daughter-in-law's blog is a great source for sharing recipes. She has many friends around the world who are excellent cooks. From one of the blog submissions I received inspiration to create this great dip. It is easy and great for gatherings.

Hot Corn Dip

- I teaspoon olive oil
- 3-4 ears of fresh corn on the cob (can use frozen if it is out of season)
- I red bell pepper, diced
- I small can of white hominy (drained)
- I small yellow onion, diced
- 2 cloves garlic, minced
- I teaspoon salt
- I teaspoon black pepper
- ¼ cup sour cream
- I chipotle pepper in adobo sauce, chopped
- I small can of olives, sliced
- I cup imitation crab pieces
- I tablespoon fresh cilantro, rough chopped
- I cup cheddar cheese, shredded, divided
- ¼ cup mayonnaise

Slice the kernels off the cob. Drizzle olive oil in a large pan and fry the corn until golden brown. Add pepper, hominy, onions, and garlic, and sauté until onions are translucent. Season the vegetables with salt and pepper. In a large bowl, mix sour cream, mayonnaise, adobo pepper, olives, crab, cilantro, and ½ of the cheese. Add vegetables to the sour cream mixture, pour into baking dish, and top with rest of cheese. Bake in a 350-degree oven for 20-25 minutes until the cheese melts and starts to brown. Enjoy with tortilla chips. Serves 6.

I love the rich color of this rice. Instead of using saffron (which is so expensive), I use annatto seed, which gives it the same color and similar flavor.

Spanish Rice

- 3 tablespoons olive oil
- I cup rice
- ½ small onion, diced
- I garlic clove, minced
- 4-5 cups chicken broth (fresh or canned)
- 3-4 stewed tomatoes (chopped)
- I small sweet pepper, diced (green, red, yellow, or chocolate)
- dash of paprika
- dash of cayenne pepper
- ½ teaspoon ground annatto seed
- ½ teaspoon salt
- ½ teaspoon black pepper
- ½ cup cheese, shredded
- 2 tablespoons fresh cilantro, roughly chopped

Heat olive oil in a skillet and sauté the onion until tender. Add garlic and the rice and fry until lightly browned over medium heat. Add rest of ingredients, cover, and cook for 30-40 minutes, stirring frequently to keep from sticking. Garnish with shredded cheese and fresh cilantro. Serves 6.

Many people think beans are beans, but I am convinced if you want really good refried beans you need to soak the pinto beans for a few days, and boil them until they are soft. Mash them and then fry them. It is then that the beans really are ready to use. I like to add a little milk, garlic, and some cotija Mexican cheese. This method takes a little time but it is well worth it.

Refried Beans

- 2 cups washed pinto beans
- ½ teaspoon baking soda
- 1 tablespoon oil
- 1 large tablespoon lard, shortening, or vegetable oil (I recommend using lard because it creates an authentic flavor)
- ½ cup milk
- 1-2 tablespoons of garlic powder
- 1 cup of crumbled cotija Mexican cheese

Soak beans completely covered in water for a few days or until tender. Once they are softened, drain the water, place the beans in a large kettle, cover with water, and add baking soda. Boil until beans are soft and can be easily mashed with a fork. Drain and mash the beans with a potato masher. Once the beans are mashed, drizzle the bottom of a fry pan with oil, add the beans, and spread mixture over the entire pan. Stir often to keep beans from burning and sticking to the bottom of the pan. Remove from heat. In a saucepan, heat shortening until it starts to smoke and then remove from the heat and add the smashed beans. Stir the mixture together. Add milk to the mixture until thinned a little. Add cheese and garlic and mix it all together until the cheese melts and the mixture is warm. Serves 8.

If you are short on time, this is a quick and easy way to make tasty refried beans from a can. Make bean dishes with ingredients right from the pantry.

Quick Refried Beans

- 1 tablespoon of lard, shortening, or vegetable oil (I recommend using lard because it creates an authentic flavor)
- 1 20-oz. can refried style beans
- ½ cup milk
- ½ cup cheese, shredded
- 1-2 teaspoons garlic powder

In a saucepan, add shortening and heat until it begins to smoke. Carefully add the can of beans and stir into the shortening. It will be a smooth texture. Turn the heat down, add milk, garlic, and heat through. Just before serving, add the cheese. Serves 4.

This is a meat-free recipe and is a great side dish. It makes a great appetizer too.

Black Bean Cakes

- 3 cloves garlic
- I small onion
- I small green pepper
- I chipotle pepper in adobo sauce
- I teaspoon cumin
- 20 black peppercorns
- I teaspoon kosher salt
- I cup flour
- I egg
- I 15-oz. can black beans, well drained

Pulse all the ingredients in a food processor. Add beans last to keep from over mashing. Form the bean mixture into small patties. Dust lightly with flour. Chill patties. Beat an egg with a wire whip until frothy. Dip each patty into egg mixture and then dust again with flour. In a fry pan, fry patties lightly on each side until the cakes are brown. Serve with Chipotle Aioli Sauce. Serves 4-6.

Chipotle Aioli Sauce

- I cup mayonnaise
- I chipotle pepper in adobo sauce
- I teaspoon garlic powder
- I teaspoon onion powder
- I teaspoon lime juice
- ½ teaspoon annatto seed powder
- ½ teaspoon black pepper
- ½ teaspoon salt
- I teaspoon cumin
- I teaspoon dried cilantro

Mix ingredients until smooth. Chill before serving. Makes 1 cup.

Black beans are loaded with antioxidants, and the meaty texture makes them a perfect side dish.

Ranch Style Black Beans

- 1 tablespoon vegetable oil
- 1 15-oz. can black beans, drained
- 2 teaspoons garlic powder
- 1 small can green chiles, diced
- 1 tomato, chopped

Mix all ingredients and heat through. Serves 4.

Asparagus is abundant in the early spring. This is a great way to bring out the nutty flavor of the vegetable.

Sonora Asparagus

- 1 lb. fresh asparagus
- 1 tablespoon olive oil
- 2 garlic cloves, crushed
- 1 teaspoon salt

Cut the asparagus into bite-size pieces. In fry pan, add olive oil, sauté garlic and asparagus until browned and tender. Add salt. Serves 4.

I have made this recipe for years and my daughter-in-law shared with me that is was her favorite. She wanted to know how to roll it out of the pan and prepare the cake for the filling. I was able to bond with my new daughter-in-law and help her make her favorite treat.

Pumpkin Cake Roll

- 3 eggs
- I cup sugar
- 2/3 cup pumpkin pie filling
- I teaspoon lemon juice
- I teaspoon baking powder
- 2 teaspoons cinnamon
- ½ teaspoon salt
- ¾ cup flour
- I cup chopped pecans (optional)

Beat eggs for 5 minutes. Add sugar to the eggs a little bit at a time. Stir in pumpkin and lemon juice. Gently fold dry ingredients into the pumpkin mixture. Grease and flour a jellyroll pan. Sprinkle pan with chopped pecans. Pour mixture into the pan. Bake at 375 degrees for 15 minutes. Turn onto a clean towel sprinkled with powdered sugar. Starting at the narrow, roll the cake and towel together and let the cake cool in the towel. Once the cake has cooled, unroll and spread with Pumpkin Roll Filling. Serves 10-12.

PUMPKIN ROLL FILLING
- ¼ cup softened margarine or butter
- I 8-oz. package cream cheese
- I cup confectioners' sugar
- I teaspoon rum flavoring
- pinch of salt

Beat the butter and cream cheese until fluffy. Add sugar. Continue beating until creamy and smooth. Add rum and salt. Spread onto the cake and roll the cake up in plastic wrap. Refrigerate. (It is easiest to slice cold.) Top with whipped cream, caramel topping, and chopped pecans.

This is a family recipe originating from my grandmother. All the ingredients are from the pantry with no need for eggs or milk. Just sweet, moist dessert you can enjoy on any outing.

Picnic Loaf Cake

- 2/3 cup raisins
- 1/3 cup dates, chopped
- 2 cups water, reserve
- 1 teaspoon baking soda
- 1 ½ cups sugar
- ½ cup shortening
- 1 teaspoon each: cloves, nutmeg, cinnamon, and allspice
- 1 cup reserved water
- 3 cups flour
- ½ teaspoon salt
- 3 teaspoons baking powder
- 1 teaspoon vanilla extract
- ½ teaspoon lemon extract

Cook raisins and dates in the water with soda until soft. Drain and reserve the water. Mix together sugar and shortening until creamy. Add spices, raisin mixture, flour, reserved water, salt, and baking powder. If the mixture gets thick, add more of the reserved water in ¼-cup increments until the dough is soft and can be poured. Bake in greased and floured medium-sized loaf pan at 350 degrees for 35-40 minutes. Makes two medium-sized loaves.

I am not sure if this is a cookie or candy. Either way I could eat the entire batch myself. It is low in fat and has very little sugar.

Coconut Date Skillet Rolls

- ¾ cup sugar
- 1 cup chopped dates
- 2 well-beaten eggs
- 1 teaspoon vanilla
- 2 cups crisp rice cereal
- 1 ½ cups flaked coconut

Combine sugar, dates, and eggs in a skillet. Cook over medium heat, stirring constantly for 5 minutes. Remove from heat and add vanilla. Carefully stir in cereal. Cool slightly, and roll into balls. While still warm, roll in coconut. Makes 24 cookies.

My favorite catering company's executive chef was raving about his flan recipe and said I needed it in my cookbook. He gave this to me and said, "It wouldn't be dessert without a flan." I love the way it makes any meal a special occasion, and it is so easy to impress your friends with an extravagant dessert without a lot of effort.

Easy Mexican Flan

- ½ cup sugar
- 1 cup milk
- 1 14-oz. can sweetened condensed milk
- 3 large egg yolks
- 1 large egg
- 1 teaspoon vanilla extract
- ½ teaspoon almond extract

In a small saucepan, melt sugar over moderate heat, stirring frequently until sugar is a dark, caramel-colored liquid. Remove from heat and pour into a 9-inch glass cake pan. Quickly turn pan to coat bottom and sides with the caramel. Let cool so caramel hardens. Heat an oven to 325 degrees.

Put the milks, eggs, and flavorings into a blender. Cover and blend to mix well. Pour mixture into the caramel-coated cake pan. Put pan into a larger pan filled with water to a depth of ½ inch. Bake for 1 hour. Remove from oven and remove mold from water. Allow the flan to come to room temperature. Run a sharp knife around the edge of the cake pan to loosen. Place a serving platter—slightly larger than the flan mold—over the mold and flip upside down. Gently remove the pan and cut the flan into wedges to serve. Serves 6.

Note: The custard should just pop right onto the platter with the luscious caramel topping dripping down the sides.

This recipe is one from a great friend who taught me how to face adversity and confront the worst situations with a sense of humor. When she got cancer, instead of hiding out and feeling miserable, she bought a pink wig and wore it proudly. She is a survivor and has kept her sense of humor through a horrible experience. I am sure there is nothing she has faced that she cannot conquer. She has been a great inspiration to me.

Oatmeal Cake

- 1 cup rolled oats
- 1 ½ cups boiling water
- 1 cube of butter
- 1 cup sugar
- 1 cup brown sugar
- 2 eggs
- 1 ½ cups flour
- 1 teaspoon salt
- 1 teaspoon soda
- 1 teaspoon cinnamon
- 2 teaspoons nutmeg

Mix oatmeal and boiling water, cover, and let sit for 20 minutes. Combine other ingredients in a separate bowl. Add oatmeal mixture to dry ingredients and blend. Bake in a greased and floured 9 x 13 pan in a 350-degree oven for 30-35 minutes. Frost the cake with the Broiled Frosting. Serves 12.

BROILED FROSTING

- 1 cube butter
- 1 cup brown sugar
- 1/3 cup evaporated milk
- 1 teaspoon vanilla
- 1 cup chopped pecans
- 1 cup coconut
- 1 teaspoon rum flavoring

Bring butter and sugar to barely a boil. Remove from heat and add vanilla, nuts, coconut, and rum, and mix. Spread mixture over the cake. Place in oven and broil until just lightly browned. Be careful—it will burn easily! Cool slightly before serving.

It was my turn to bring dessert to the family Thanksgiving celebration, so I adapted an existing cheesecake recipe to pumpkin. Everyone loved it!

Pumpkin Cheesecake

CRUST

- 1 ½ cups ginger cookie crumbs
- ¼ cup sugar
- 1 tablespoon orange juice
- 1 teaspoon nutmeg
- 1/3 cup melted butter

FILLING

- 2 8-oz. packages softened cream cheese
- 1 cup sugar
- 3 eggs
- ½ cup sour cream
- 1 ½ cups canned pumpkin
- ½ teaspoon cinnamon
- ½ teaspoon ginger
- ½ teaspoon salt
- ¼ teaspoon nutmeg
- 1 teaspoon orange juice

Heat an oven to 350 degrees. Spray bottom of 9-inch springform pan with cooking spray. Do not spray sides. Mix all crust ingredients. Press evenly over the bottom and ½ inch up the sides of the pan. Bake 10 minutes. Beat cream cheese and sugar until smooth. Add eggs one at a time, beating just until combined. (Make sure the cream cheese and eggs are room temperature—they beat better.) Beat in sour cream, pumpkin, and spices. Pour into pan. Wrap outside of pan with heavy foil so water won't seep in while baking. Place pan in large, shallow roasting pan. Fill roasting pan with enough hot water to come up ½ inch up the sides of the springform pan. Bake 65 minutes or until edges are puffed and top looks dull and is dry to the touch. Center should be less set than the edges. Remove from oven and remove from pan of water. Cool completely on wire rack. Refrigerate at least 4 hours or overnight before serving. Drizzle cheesecake with Orange Sauce and a dollop of whipped cream before serving. Serves 12.

Orange Sauce

- ½ cup butter
- 1 cup packed dark brown sugar
- ½ cup whipping cream
- 1 tablespoon vanilla extract
- 1 teaspoon orange juice
- 1 teaspoon rum flavoring

Melt butter and whisk in brown sugar until mixture is smooth. Whisk in whipping cream, vanilla, orange juice, and rum. Bring to a boil and cool completely. Drizzle over cheesecake. Makes 1 cup.

Sopapillas are like a donut or beignet. They are a tender, sweet treat that you can fill with honey or jelly. If you like churros, you will love these treats.

Sopapillas

- 4 cups flour
- 1 teaspoon salt
- 2 teaspoons baking powder
- 4 tablespoons shortening
- 4 eggs
- ½ cup sugar
- ¾ cup watered-down milk
- ¾ cup honey or jelly
- ½ cup sugar
- 3 teaspoons cinnamon
- small paper bag

Mix flour with salt and baking powder. Cut the shortening into the dry ingredients. In separate bowl beat the eggs and add sugar. Add the flour mixture to the eggs and sugar mixture. Add enough watered-down milk to make medium dough. Let dough rest for 30 minutes. On a floured surface, roll dough to ¼-inch thick and cut into 2-inch squares. Place a ½ teaspoon of jelly in center of dough. Fold one corner of dough over jelly and pinch down to seal. They will look like small turnovers. Fry in deep fat at 375 degrees until golden brown. Drain on a paper towel lined plate. Place sugar and cinnamon in a small bag and shake the sugar seasoning to coat each Sopapilla. Makes 2-3 dozen.

Bertha is 90 years young and has taught our neighborhood the art of candy making. This is her most famous recipe. After tasting it, I can see why. It is a great flavor combination.

Licorice Caramel

- 1 14-oz. can of sweetened condensed milk
- 1 ½ cups white corn syrup
- 1 cup white sugar
- 1 cup butter
- ¼ teaspoon salt
- 1 teaspoon black food-coloring paste
- 1 ½ teaspoons anise oil
- 2 tablespoons sea salt or kosher salt, divided

Cook all ingredients on medium heat, stirring constantly until it boils. Add food-coloring paste. Cook while stirring to 234 degrees on a candy thermometer. Remove from heat and add anise oil. Pour into a buttered and salted 9 x 11 pan. Salt the top of candy. Cool. Cut and wrap in waxed paper. Makes 48 candies.

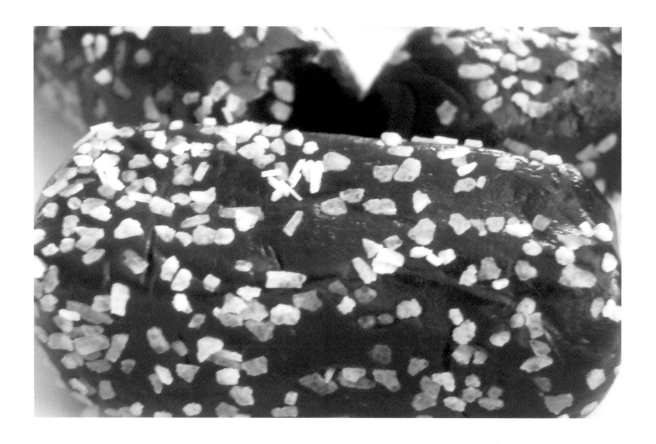

I think there are versions of this cookie in every culture. Bite-sized shortbread cookies are perfect for parties. I serve them every year at my holiday party. Guests just pop them in their mouths. My version has just a hint of orange.

Wedding Cookies

- 2 ½ cups flour
- 1 teaspoon ground cinnamon
- 1 teaspoon grated orange zest
- 1 cup softened butter
- 1 cup finely chopped pecans
- ½ cup confectioners' sugar
- 1 ½ teaspoon vanilla extract
- extra small bowl of powdered sugar

In large bowl, combine all ingredients. Stir well. Using your hands, shape dough into 1-inch diameter balls. Bake on an ungreased baking sheet in a 400-degree oven for 10-12 minutes. While the cookies are warm, roll balls in powdered sugar. Once they are cool, roll in powdered sugar again. Makes 24 cookies.

My sister, Toni, makes the best caramel popcorn. It is ooey and gooey and ever so addicting. She makes it with a product called corn puffs. Do not confuse it with cereal. You buy it in the chips aisle and it is readily available in most grocery stores. Pour the caramel sauce over the entire bag. If you cannot find corn puffs...popcorn works very well too.

Caramel Corn Puffs

- 2 ¼ cups brown sugar
- 1 cup light corn syrup
- 1 cube of butter
- 1 14-oz. can sweetened condensed milk
- 1 teaspoon vanilla
- 1 large bag corn puffs or 5 cups popped popcorn

Dissolve sugar and corn syrup in a saucepan over medium heat. Once dissolved, bring to a boil and remove from heat. Add butter, return to the heat, and bring to a boil. Remove from heat and add milk. Return the pan to the heat and bring to a boil, stirring constantly. Remove from heat and add vanilla. Pour over a large bowl of corn puffs or popcorn and gently stir until all morsels are touched with the caramel sauce. Serves 12.

If I had to choose between date bars and brownies, it would be a hard decision. They are both so good. When you are not in a chocolate mood, try the date bars.

Date Bars with Orange Cream Icing

BARS

- ¼ cup softened butter
- ½ cup packed brown sugar
- I egg
- 2 teaspoons orange zest, divided and reserved
- I cup flour
- ½ teaspoon baking powder
- ¼ teaspoon baking soda
- ¼ cup orange juice
- ¼ cup milk
- ½ cup chopped and pitted dates
- ½ cup chopped pecans or walnuts (optional)

In a large mixing bowl, beat butter for 30 seconds. Add brown sugar, egg, and orange zest; beat until creamy. Add dry ingredients. Mix the orange juice and the milk together and then add to the mixture alternatively. Stir in the dates and nuts. Spread onto a 9 x 11 baking dish. Bake at 350 degrees for 12-15 minutes or until done. The bar will pull from the sides of the pan and the center will be set. Cool. Frost bars with Orange Cream Cheese Icing and garnish with reserved orange zest. Cut into squares to serve. Makes 24 bars.

Orange Cream Cheese Icing

- ½ cup softened butter or margarine
- I 8-oz. package cream cheese
- 2 cups confectioners' sugar
- milk to moisten
- I teaspoon vanilla
- I teaspoon orange zest

In mixer, whip butter and cream cheese until smooth. Add powdered sugar and milk to moisten to desired texture. Add vanilla and orange zest for flavor. Spread over date bars. Makes 2 cups.

My childhood friend Kimberly would share with me pumpkin treats made by her grandmother from Mexico. They tasted similar to a pumpkin-flavored candy. It was a yummy treat and a flavor I would crave. I now suppress the craving with Pumpkin Chocolate Chip Cookies.

Pumpkin Chocolate Chip Cookies

- ½ cup butter or margarine
- ¼ cup shortening
- ¾ cup brown sugar
- ¾ cup white sugar
- 1 egg
- 1 cup canned pumpkin
- 1/3 cup molasses
- 1 teaspoon vanilla extract
- 3 cups flour, divided
- 1 teaspoon baking powder
- 1 teaspoon soda
- 1 teaspoon salt
- ½ teaspoon ground nutmeg
- 1 teaspoon cinnamon
- ½ teaspoon ground cloves
- 1 cup chocolate chips
- ½ cup chopped nuts (optional)

In a large bowl, cream the sugars and butter together. Add the egg and beat until fluffy. Add pumpkin, molasses, and vanilla. Add ½ of the flour and other dry ingredients. Mix until blended. Add remaining flour, chocolate chips, and nuts. Blend well. Place in the refrigerator until slightly chilled. Preheat oven to 350 degrees. Place wax paper on cookie sheets. Change the paper between batches. Drop by spoonful onto the cookie sheet and bake for 11-12 minutes. Do not over bake. Cookies will look slightly underdone. Cool on wire racks or brown paper. Makes 48 cookies.

Everyone asks Liz to bake cookies and other pastries when they have a special occasion. She cheerfully agrees to share her baking talent. When she offered me her fabulous Zucchini Bread recipe for my cookbook, I jumped at the chance. It is similar to many others but just a little sweeter, like Liz.

Zucchini Bread

- 3 eggs
- I cup vegetable oil
- 2 ½ cups sugar
- 2 cups zucchini squash, peeled, grated
- I tablespoon vanilla
- 3 cups flour
- I-teaspoon salt
- I teaspoon baking soda
- ¼ teaspoon baking powder
- I tablespoon cinnamon
- ½ cup nuts, chopped (optional)
- ½ cup chocolate chips (optional)

Beat eggs and add oil, sugar, zucchini, and vanilla. Mix well. Add flour, salt, soda, baking powder, and cinnamon. Add the nuts and chocolate chips last. Mix well and pour into greased and floured loaf pans. Do not fill the pans up because the dough will rise and overflow, about 2/3rds is best. Bake 50-60 minutes at 350 degrees. Makes 3 large loaf pans. I keep peeled and shredded zucchini from the garden frozen in the freezer for easy convenience. Defrost and drain before using.

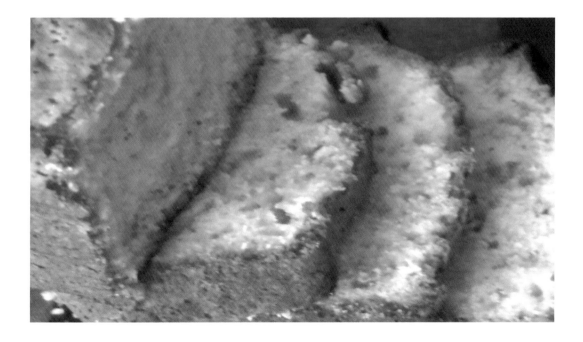

This recipe is a great way to satisfy a sweet tooth and your resolution to eat more fruits.

Kickin' Fruit Platter

- 1 whole pineapple, peeled
- 1 cantaloupe, peeled
- 1 honeydew melon, peeled

Slice pineapple, cantaloupe, and honeydew melon into bite-sized pieces and arrange on a platter. Drizzle the fruit with Jalapeño Syrup and serve. Serves 6.

Jalapeño Syrup

- 2 cups sugar
- 1 cup water
- 1 teaspoon jalapeño juice

Cook water and sugar in a saucepan until sugar dissolves and the syrup comes to a boil. Boil for 1 minute. Remove from heat and add jalapeño juice. Let cool before pouring over the fruit. Makes 1 cup.

If you have ever grown zucchini in a vegetable garden and experienced the abundance, this is a delicious way to use the squash. I like to put this in a bundt cake pan and then frost it with Easy Chocolate Glaze.

Chocolate Zucchini Bundt Cake

- ¾ cup margarine or butter
- 2 cups sugar
- 3 eggs
- 2 teaspoons vanilla
- 2 cups peeled and grated zucchini squash
- 1 ½ cups milk
- 2 ½ cups flour
- 1 ½ cups cocoa
- 2 ½ teaspoons baking powder
- 1 ½ teaspoons baking soda
- 1 teaspoon salt
- 1 teaspoon cinnamon
- ½ teaspoon chili powder

Cream the butter and sugar together. Add eggs one at a time, beating until fluffy each time. Add vanilla, zucchini, and milk alternately with the dry ingredients. Pour into a greased baking pan and bake at 350 degrees until test stick comes out clean. Cool. Spoon glaze mixture over entire cake until entire cake is covered. Refrigerate so the chocolate sets. Serve at room temperature. Serves 8.

Easy Chocolate Glaze

- ½ of a 12-oz. bag of chocolate chips
- 6 tablespoons butter
- dash of cinnamon
- dash of chili powder
- 1 teaspoon vanilla

Melt chocolate chips and butter in microwave for about 1 minute, stirring until the chocolate is smooth. After the first minute, cook at 30-second intervals to avoid overheating. Add vanilla, chili powder, and cinnamon. Makes 1 cup.

A variety of cookies and candies are part of the Christmas holiday. Along with all the Mexican goodies, I like to add a few of my personal favorites. This is one of my mother's recipes and I love the contrast of ingredients.

Thumbprint Cookies

- ½ cup butter
- ½ cup shortening
- ½ cup packed brown sugar
- 2 eggs, separated
- I teaspoon vanilla
- 2 cups flour
- ½ teaspoon salt
- I ½ cups chopped walnuts
- I small jar mint jelly

Heat an oven to 350 degrees. Mix thoroughly the butter, shortening, sugar, egg yolk, and vanilla. Mix in flour and salt until the dough holds together and can be handled. Shape into ½ inch balls. In separate bowl beat the egg whites slightly. Dip each dough ball into the egg white and then roll in the nuts. Place once inch apart on ungreased baking sheet. Press thumb deeply into center of each ball. Bake about 10 minutes or until a light brown. Immediately remove from baking sheet and cool on wire racks. Fill each cookie with a teaspoon of mint jelly. Makes 36 cookies.

LaVergne, TN USA
26 March 2010
177234LV00001B